DWIGHT D. *Eisenhower*

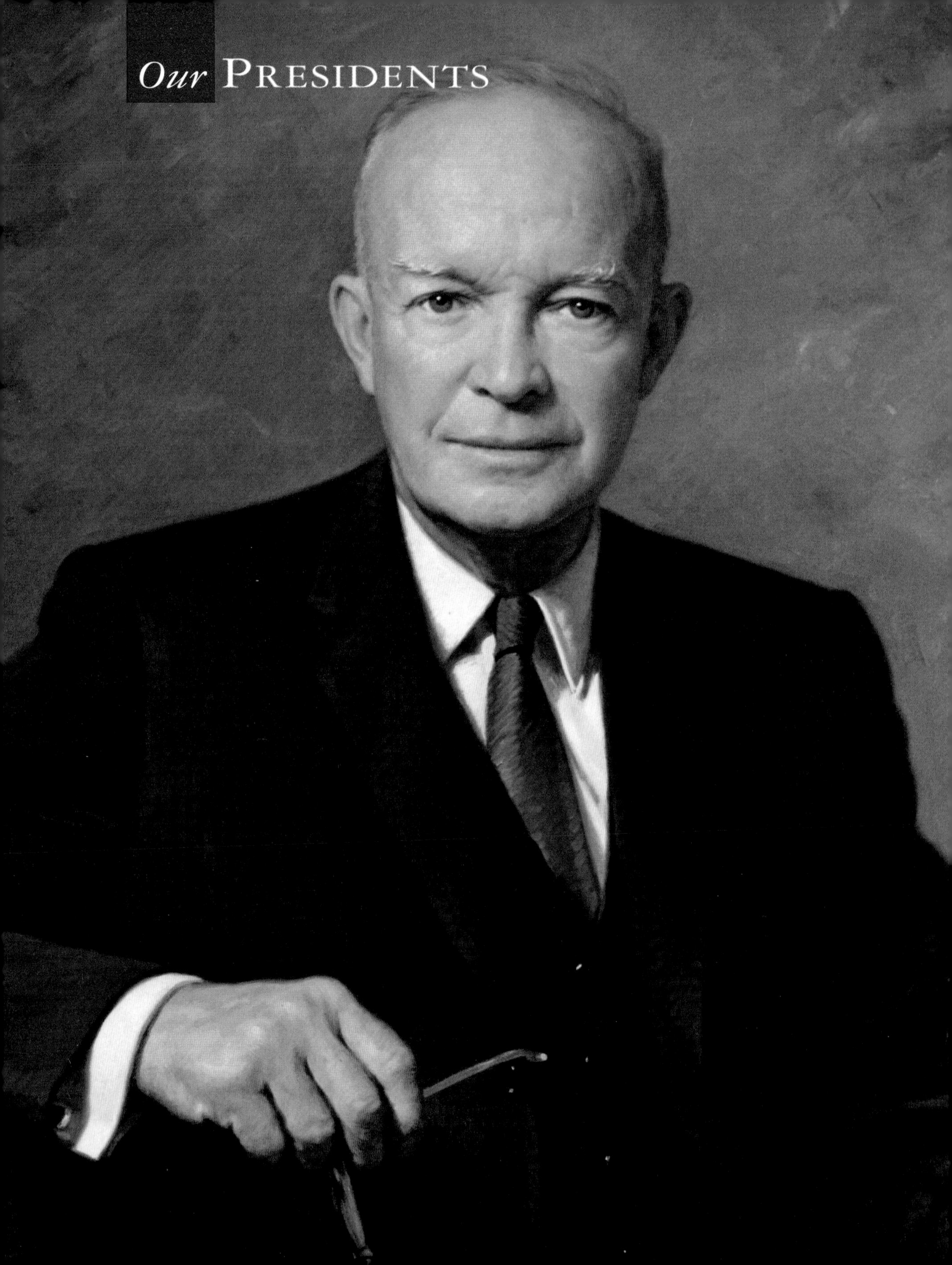

Dwight D. *Eisenhower*

OUR THIRTY-FOURTH PRESIDENT

By Sarah Bowler

SPIRIT
of America™

The Child's World®, Inc.
Chanhassen, Minnesota

6

Dwight D. *Eisenhower*

Published in the United States of America by The Child's World®, Inc.
PO Box 326 • Chanhassen, MN 55317-0326 • 800-599-READ • www.childsworld.com

Acknowledgments
The Creative Spark: Mary Francis-DeMarois, Project Director; Elizabeth Sirimarco Budd, Series Editor; Robert Court, Design and Art Direction; Janine Graham, Page Layout; Jennifer Moyers, Production

The Child's World®, Inc.: Mary Berendes, Publishing Director; Red Line Editorial, Fact Research; Cindy Klingel, Curriculum Advisor; Robert Noyed, Historical Advisor

Photos
Cover: White House Collection, courtesy White House Historical Association; Corbis: 29; Courtesy of the Dwight D. Eisenhower Library, Abilene, Texas: 6, 7, 8, 10, 11, 12, 13, 14, 15, 16, 19, 22, 23, 24, 25, 27, 30, 36; Courtesy of the Franklin D. Roosevelt Library and Museum: 17, 18; Library of Congress: 20, 21, 26, 28, 31, 33, 34, 37

Registration
The Child's World®, Inc., Spirit of America™, and their associated logos are the sole property and registered trademarks of The Child's World®, Inc.

Library of Congress Cataloging-in-Publication Data
Bowler, Sarah. 1949–
    Dwight D. Eisenhower, our thirty-fourth president / by Sarah Bowler.
        p. cm. Includes bibliographical references and index.
    ISBN 1-56766-868-2 (lib. bdg. : alk. paper)
    1. Eisenhower, Dwight D. (Dwight David), 1890–1969—Juvenile literature.
    2. Presidents—United States—Biography—Juvenile literature. [1. Eisenhower, Dwight D. (Dwight David), 1890–1969. 2. Presidents.]   I. Title.
    E836 .B69 2001
    973.921'092—dc21

                                                        00-010935

Contents

Chapter ONE

A Military Path

As children, Dwight and his brothers were expected to help their family. "Always you had a responsibility to do something," he said. "And it could be scrubbing the floors on Saturday morning, it could be washing the dishes, or it could be taking care of the horses or the cows or the chickens."

DWIGHT DAVID EISENHOWER WAS ALWAYS a fighter. But whether he was involved in neighborhood scuffles, high school football games, World War II invasions, or important decisions as president of the United States, his great gift was the ability to bring people together to work as a team.

Dwight was born in Denison, Texas, on October 14, 1890. He was the third of David and Ida Eisenhower's seven sons. When he was almost two years old, the family moved to Abilene, Kansas.

Dwight had a happy childhood and later wrote, "If we were poor, we were unaware of it … we were a cheerful and vital family." He was aware, however, of the rivalry between the boys on the south side of town (where he lived),

and the boys on the north side (where the richer families lived). Sometimes the north-side boys teased Dwight about his tattered clothing or hand-me-down shoes. He often got into fights, and was known as a good fighter with an angry temper. Dwight's mother did not approve of his fighting, however. Ida Eisenhower was a pacifist, a person who believes in peace. She encouraged her son to find other ways to solve his problems.

Dwight's family did not have much money, but they were happy, hardworking, and honest. They lived in a small, simple home made of clapboard. Dwight (at far left) later remembered that his childhood home had less floor space than his office at the Pentagon, the U.S. military headquarters in Washington, D.C.

As a boy, Dwight (center) lived in a small town. He enjoyed all the benefits that life in the country could provide. He spent time outdoors, fishing and hunting in the nearby wilderness. He also enjoyed going camping with his friends. He is shown here on a 1907 camping trip.

One day, Dwight thought he had been treated unfairly. He was so angry that he ran up to an apple tree and began punching it with his fists. "I was there crying as hard as I could and beating this tree with my fists, and they were all bleeding and messy," he later recalled. Dwight's father sent him to his room. His mother came to him and nursed his hands. Then she said he must learn how to keep from hurting himself. Dwight remembered this as an important moment in his life. "Since then I've gotten angry many times, but I have tried to keep from showing it."

In high school, Dwight turned his competitive spirit to sports. During his senior year, he became a star football player. His favorite subject at school was American history. "Since those early years," he later said, "history of all kinds, and certainly political and military, has always intrigued me."

When he graduated from high school, Ike, as he was called, couldn't afford the

8

tuition for college. After working for two years, he was admitted to West Point Military Academy, where the government would pay for his college education. Ike was thrilled at this opportunity, but it was difficult for his mother to see him go. She knew he would become a soldier, and she hated to think of him going to war. Ike's youngest brother told him how she had wept after he left for West Point. Ike knew that his mother was worried about his future. "She was very religious," he remembered later. "She believed that violence was wicked and wrong." Although Ike would be a soldier for much of his life, his mother's beliefs would always have a strong influence on him. He believed that the nation should strive for peace whenever possible.

Team sports were important at West Point. They taught cooperation and teamwork, and these were good qualities for soldiers to have. Football was Ike's main interest, and he was an outstanding player. He was terribly disappointed when injuries ended his football career, but he went on to graduate with the class of 1915.

Ike's first assignment was at Fort Sam Houston, Texas. There he met Mamie Geneva

Ike loved sports. He played both football and baseball at Abilene High School. He played football at West Point during his second year there. After a knee injury forced him to quit playing, he assisted the team's coaching staff.

Doud, the daughter of a wealthy family from Denver, Colorado. Ike and Mamie began seeing a lot of each other, and soon fell in love. Since Mamie loved parties and pretty clothes, some of her friends thought Ike was too poor for her. But Mamie didn't care. She and Ike were married on July 1, 1916.

Soon after that, the United States was at war. Germany had been fighting with other European countries for several years in what later became known as World War I. The Germans were using their submarines to sink ships from other nations, including the United States. In 1917, President Woodrow Wilson asked the U.S. Congress to declare war on Germany, marking the beginning of America's role in World War I.

Ike was ordered to Camp Colt, near Gettysburg, Pennsylvania. His job was to train soldiers to use a new weapon, the armored tank. Unfortunately, they had no tanks. Ike had to train his men using boxes. He did his

10

job so well under these difficult conditions that he later received a medal.

With the war over, Ike was transferred to Camp Meade, Maryland. There he met General Fox Conner, who was convinced that there would soon be another major war. He urged Ike to continue his studies of military history. This would help him understand war **strategy** to make him a better leader.

During the next few years, Ike was assigned to various military bases in the United States and in France. He remembered General Conner's prediction and decided to attend a special army college in Fort Leavenworth, Kansas. Ike graduated at the top of his class of 275 students. Later, he studied at the Army War College in Washington, D.C.

In France, Ike's jobs were to write a guide to World War I battlefields and to study the French countryside—the terrain, railroads, and highways. He didn't know how useful this information would be to him later, when he led the invasion of France in World War II.

In 1933, Ike became an aide to General Douglas MacArthur, the U.S. Army's chief of staff. Two years later, he went with MacArthur

As a boy, Dwight had always thought he would become a railroad engineer. But then he passed the exam that allowed him to attend West Point, the U.S. Army's college, free of charge. He graduated from West Point on June 12, 1915, and began a long and honorable military career.

▶ In 1919, Ike was assigned to an army experiment to see how long it would take to drive a long line of trucks, called a convoy, across the United States. Driving as fast as possible, it took two months to travel from Washington, D.C., to San Francisco. Years later, when Ike became president, he began a program to build a system of interstate highways. Today these roads make it possible to drive from coast to coast without ever stopping at a traffic light, making the trip much quicker.

Ike is shown here inspecting trenches dug by a unit of soldiers. During World War I, soldiers fought from trenches like these that were dug several feet into the ground.

to work in the Philippines. By the end of the 1930s, it was clear that General Conner's prediction of another global war was coming true. In 1940, Ike left MacArthur to become involved in the war preparations. He had missed a chance to fight in World War I, but in the years since, his military path had prepared him to play a major role in World War II.

IKE AND MAMIE EISENHOWER posed for this wedding portrait in 1916. After they were married, they lived in a small apartment at Fort Sam Houston. Ike and Mamie liked to have friends over for dinner and to play cards. In fact, they had so many parties, their friends called their home "Club Eisenhower."

Their first child, Doud Dwight, was born in September of 1917. The family lived together at Camp Meade, Maryland, where the baby became a favorite of the soldiers in Ike's unit. They had a little uniform made for him and sometimes took him on drills. When his son died in early 1921 of a serious illness called scarlet fever, it was the greatest tragedy of Ike's life. Little Doud was just over three years old.

Their second son, John Sheldon Doud Eisenhower, was born in August of 1922. As John grew older, he enjoyed talking to his father and going with him to work. They also played tennis together, and John usually won. Ike was delighted when John decided to attend West Point and pursue a career in the army.

Ike's frequent moves throughout his military career kept him away from his family much of the time, but he was happiest when they were all together.

Chapter TWO

A Great General

Eisenhower, shown here at the end of World War II, was a great military leader. But he also knew the cost of war. "I hate war as only a soldier who has lived it can, only as one who has seen its brutality, its stupidity."

BY THE TIME EISENHOWER RETURNED TO the United States, World War II had already begun. After the previous World War, Germany struggled to recover. Its people faced poverty. Then the Nazi Party came to power in the early 1930s. The Nazis blamed other countries for the difficulties that Germany faced. They also blamed the Jewish people, who they claimed were destroying Germany. The Nazis promised to make things better, even if it meant another war—and the violent removal of all Jews from Europe.

By 1939, the Germans had invaded Poland. Then England and France declared war on the Germans. It seemed that the United States would not be able to stay out of the war forever. To prepare, the U.S. began building up

In 1940, Eisenhower (second from left) was sent to Washington to work with other military leaders at the War Department. They created strategies to help the United States fight World War II. Soon the army would send him to Europe to direct troops.

its military forces. Once back in the United States, Eisenhower trained soldiers and practiced war **maneuvers.** He was so good at the job that he was **promoted** to brigadier general.

In Europe, the Germans were winning the war. By 1940, they had already conquered Holland, Belgium, Luxembourg, and most of France. The Nazis were bombing London every day. The British were fighting desperately to hold out against them.

On the other side of the world, Japan was attacking Asian countries. It had invaded China in 1937. By 1939, it was trying to gain more territory in East Asia. The United States paid

Interesting Facts

▶ General Eisenhower was not a formal man. He once said that when the soldiers called him Ike, "I knew everything was going well."

▸ In the weeks before D-Day, General Eisenhower spent all the time he could visiting the troops all over England. He wanted to encourage them with the importance of their mission to stop Adolf Hitler and the Nazi Party.

▸ On the day General Eisenhower was leading the D-Day invasion, his son, John, was graduating from West Point. Later that summer, John arrived in Europe to visit his father. General Eisenhower took him everywhere, including the battlefront. Although John pleaded with his father to let him join a combat unit in France, this was against army rules.

little attention to the problems there until December 7, 1941.

On that day, Japan attacked Pearl Harbor in Hawaii. Thousands of Americans were killed and injured, and several U.S. battleships were destroyed. The next day, the United States declared war on Japan. Germany and Italy then declared war on the United States on December 11.

Within a week of the attack, the U.S. Army chief of staff, General George G. Marshall, ordered Eisenhower to report to Washington. There he would help with war strategy. Marshall was so impressed with Eisenhower, he promoted him to major general. In 1942, he was appointed commander of all the American troops in Europe, with the rank of lieutenant general.

German victories were mounting. They had conquered most of Europe and were gaining vast areas of Russian territory. In the south, German tank units were moving across North Africa.

The **Allies,** as the countries fighting against the Germans were called, decided to invade North Africa first. Eisenhower's headquarters were under the Rock of Gibraltar at the western

16

end of the Mediterranean Sea. From there, he directed the landing of Allied troops on North African beaches in November of 1942. By 1943, they had taken much of North Africa from the Nazis.

Eisenhower ordered his troops back onto the ships. They sailed across the Mediterranean and quickly conquered the Italian island of Sicily, which is off the country's southern coast. Allied forces then invaded Italy's mainland. The Italian government surrendered almost immediately.

Finally, the Allies were winning battles. Eisenhower was rewarded with a promotion to four-star general, the second highest rank in the army. He was put in charge of the biggest Allied attack of all, the invasion of **occupied** France.

Eisenhower knew it was important that soldiers from all the Allied countries see themselves as part of a single fighting force.

On December 7, 1941, the Japanese bombed Pearl Harbor in Hawaii. This act killed 2,403 Americans and wounded more than a thousand. The next day, the United States declared war. "No matter how long it may take us," President Franklin D. Roosevelt stated in a radio speech, "the American people in their righteous might will win through to absolute victory." Eisenhower's great skill as a leader would be an important part of this victory.

He worked with British, French, and other Allied leaders to plan the enormous attack, called "Operation Overlord." The secret date of the attack was referred to as "D-Day." Eisenhower was named the supreme commander of this mission, in charge of all the Allied troops.

After Eisenhower and his troops captured the island of Sicily, President Franklin D. Roosevelt (right) traveled there to congratulate them. That day, the president told Eisenhower what an important role he was about to play in the war. "Well, Ike, you are going to command Operation Overlord."

Allied forces had planned the invasion for two years. Ships brought millions of tons of weapons and equipment to England. As D-Day approached, about 5,000 ships and 1,200 airplanes were ready for the attack. Eisenhower was responsible for all the equipment and for the nearly three million troops who played a role in the invasion.

The soldiers loved Eisenhower. He inspired them with his sincerity and easy discipline. He wanted to build their morale, the spirit and enthusiasm of people working together toward a common goal. He considered the troops' morale to be "the greatest single factor in successful war."

On the morning of D-Day, June 6, 1944, the first troops landed on the shores of France. Nazi soldiers were taken by surprise. By the end of the first day, Allied troops had captured a long stretch of beach. In one day, 132,000 troops and 23,000 paratroopers landed in France. Paratroopers are soldiers that are dropped from airplanes and parachute into enemy territory. Within a month, more than a million Allied soldiers had landed in Europe. They were joined by thousands of soldiers from the French underground, who were ready to fight the Nazis. The underground was made up of French citizens who secretly fought the pro-German government that ruled France during World War II.

As supreme commander of Operation Overlord, General Eisenhower was in charge of the enormous D-Day invasion, shown here. Eisenhower reported the victory, saying, "The Allied force, which invaded Europe on June 6, has utterly defeated the Germans by land, sea, and air."

General Eisenhower is shown here in New York City during a victory parade. After the war in Europe ended, he was considered a great hero. But Eisenhower did not want to take credit for the hard-fought victory. "I am not a hero," Ike later said, "I am the symbol of the heroic men you people, and all the United States, have sent to war."

In less than a year, Nazi troops had been pushed back to Germany. They were soon killed or captured by Allied forces. Germany surrendered on May 7, 1945.

Operation Overlord was the largest invasion in the history of the world. Its success was the greatest achievement of Ike's military career. He was hailed as a great hero in the United States, Great Britain, France, and in all the other Allied countries.

Later, in 1945, President Harry S. Truman called Eisenhower to Washington to become chief of staff of the U.S. Army. Now a five-star general, he was the head of all the armed forces.

ADOLF HITLER WAS THE LEADER OF THE NAZI **POLITICAL PARTY.** IN 1933, he became the dictator of Germany, a ruler with complete power over the country. He built up Germany's military. Then he began to take over the surrounding countries. The Germans occupied Austria in 1938, then Czechoslovakia in 1939. When the Nazis invaded Poland in September of 1939, France and Great Britain declared war. The Soviet Union entered the war after Germany invaded it in 1941.

Hitler and the leaders of Italy and Japan had agreed to work together. They called themselves the Axis powers. Japan had invaded China in 1937, but it was not until the Japanese bombed Pearl Harbor in 1941 that the United States became involved in the war. Eisenhower was not involved in the war in Japan, but led the Allies in Europe and Africa.

The full extent of what the Allies were fighting for became clear after Germany surrendered on May 7, 1945. Liberating troops were horrified to find death camps in which more than six million Jewish people had been worked to death or murdered. Hitler and the Nazis had blamed them for Germany's problems and intended to destroy the Jewish race.

The war with Japan ended after the United States dropped **atomic bombs** on the Japanese cities of Hiroshima and Nagasaki. These acts instantly killed many thousands of people. The Japanese surrendered on August 14, 1945. World War II was over.

From War Hero to President

As the army's chief of staff, Eisenhower focused on demobilization, or the disbanding of the armed forces after the war. In 1948, he retired from active duty to become the president of Columbia University in New York City. He continued to advise the government on military matters.

One of the problems that appeared after World War II was the rise of **communism.** In communist countries, citizens do not own land and businesses. Instead, everything is owned and run by the government and belongs to the country as a whole. The Soviet Union had been a communist country since 1917. Its leaders believed in an all-powerful state with only one political party. The Soviet people did not have elections. They also had

no personal freedoms, such as freedom of speech or the freedom to practice a religion.

After World War II, the Soviet Union occupied Eastern Europe. It set up communist governments in many countries there. Soon it became a powerful empire. This power and the communist ideals posed a threat to **democracies.** In response, the United States, Canada, and the nations of Western Europe created the North Atlantic Treaty Organization (NATO). This was a military alliance meant to guard against communist attack.

In 1950, President Harry Truman asked Eisenhower to go to Europe as the supreme commander of NATO. His job would be to

In 1950, President Harry Truman sent Eisenhower back to Europe as the supreme commander of NATO troops.

Interesting Facts

▸ Eisenhower was the first president to be born in Texas.

▸ On June 7, 1955, Eisenhower became the first president to be shown on television in color.

23

Before the election of 1952, Eisenhower and the vice presidential candidate, Richard Nixon, appeared at many events. Eisenhower told people that he would be an honest president. "I'm going to try to be just as truthful as I can be," he said.

organize a military force of soldiers from the 11 NATO countries. They would then be prepared to defend Europe against Soviet attack. Even though Eisenhower had retired from active duty, he was still dedicated to his country. "I'm a soldier," he said, "and if you ask me to go, of course, I will go."

While he was in Europe with NATO, many people urged Eisenhower to run for president. Finally, he agreed to be the Republican Party **candidate.** The Republicans are one of the country's two most powerful political parties. Upon returning to the United

States, Eisenhower chose Richard M. Nixon, a U.S. senator from California, to run for vice president. On November 4, 1952, Eisenhower defeated Adlai Stevenson by more than six million votes.

While Eisenhower was running for president, one of the most important issues had been the Korean War. Korea had divided into two countries: North Korea, which was communist, and South Korea, which was not. In 1950, North Korea had attacked South Korea. Many people thought this proved that the communists were trying to spread their ideas around the world. The United States and other countries sent troops to help South Korea.

During the Korean War, American soldiers traveled to Asia to protect South Korea. Eisenhower visited Korea before he became president.

China and the Soviet Union sent ground and air forces to support the North Koreans. A bloody war raged between the two sides. Before the election, Eisenhower promised to help end the war as soon as possible.

Six months after Eisenhower became president, the Korean War ended. Even though the war was over, millions of Americans now believed that communist governments were trying to take over the world.

In the 1950s, Senator Joseph McCarthy accused many Americans of supporting communism. Often what he said was wrong or unfair. But at the time, Americans were afraid that the Soviets planned to take over the country. McCarthy was able to convince people that communism was already a serious threat in the United States.

A U.S. senator named Joseph McCarthy used the fear of communism to gain power in politics. He accused many writers, actors, politicians, and other American citizens of being communists. He said they were a threat to the safety of the United States. Many of those he branded as communists had their careers ruined. Americans began to worry that whatever they said against the U.S. government could be used against them. This movement to accuse people of being communist became known as "McCarthyism." It went against one of the most basic rights of American citizens: freedom of speech.

Some people criticized Eisenhower for not stopping McCarthy. Senator McCarthy had traveled on Eisenhower's campaign train. Back in 1950, Richard Nixon, who became Eisenhower's vice president, had supported McCarthy's anti-communist movement. He had hoped this would help him get elected to the Senate. But Eisenhower said he didn't want to interfere with Congress. Finally, McCarthy went too far. He began accusing people in the U.S. Army. In 1954, the Senate voted to **censure** Senator McCarthy for his actions.

President Eisenhower did not feel that McCarthyism was necessary to protect the United States. Still, concerns about the spread of communism were serious during his presidency. In 1955, the leaders of France, Great Britain, the Soviet Union, and the United States met in Switzerland. Both the United States and the Soviet Union had atomic bombs. These nuclear weapons were capable

During the 1952 presidential campaign, Mamie Eisenhower did whatever she could to help her husband. She listened to his speeches and offered suggestions to improve them. She also answered the letters she received from his supporters.

Interesting Facts

▶ During Eisenhower's first term, the minimum wage allowed by law was raised to $1.00 an hour.

After his heart attack in 1955, President Eisenhower stayed in Colorado until his health improved. But he let newspapers publish photographs of him to show the American people that he was doing well.

of destroying much of the world. President Eisenhower and Russia's leader, Nikita Khrushchev, knew they must avoid war. Eisenhower suggested that the two nations should allow each other to fly over their military bases. This way, neither country would worry about secret military strength. Khrushchev didn't like this "Open Skies" policy. He said the United States wanted to spy on the Soviet Union.

These distrustful feelings between the United States and the Soviet Union became known as the "Cold War." For years, people in both countries were afraid that nuclear bombs might one day cause widespread destruction and death.

In September of 1955, Eisenhower had a heart attack while he was on vacation in Denver, Colorado. Members of his staff went to Denver and carried on the president's work. By February of 1956, Eisenhower had recovered. He announced that he planned to run for a second **term.** In November, he again defeated Adlai Stevenson.

MANY MIDDLE-CLASS AMERICANS HAD COMFORTABLE LIVES IN THE 1950S. In 1954, President Eisenhower urged Congress to pass a **bill** that would allow Americans to pay fewer **taxes.** Businesses could grow larger, and the nation could grow richer. There were more good jobs available than ever before. People had money to spend, and many bought new homes in the suburbs, areas on the outskirts of cities. New houses had been built for the millions of soldiers returning from World War II. They needed new roads, cars, and schools. Building these things created even more jobs. Americans bought electric appliances for their modern kitchens and lawn mowers for their new yards. On television, a recent invention, people watched advertisements for all the things they could buy. Americans went on a spending spree, and manufacturers produced what they wanted. For many, the 1950s were successful years, a time of prosperity.

Chapter FOUR

The Second Term

President Eisenhower always seemed to be relaxed and smiling. His years in the White House seemed peaceful, although there were problems both at home and abroad.

As Eisenhower began his second term, **racial** tension flared in the United States. In 1954, the Supreme Court had ruled that public schools had to be **integrated**. This meant that public schools had to accept students of all races. In 1957, nine African American students planned to test that ruling by attending an all-white high school in Little Rock, Arkansas.

Governor Orval Faubus ordered the Arkansas National Guard to prevent the black students from entering the school. President Eisenhower demanded that Faubus enforce the Supreme Court decision. He said Faubus must allow the students to attend the high school. The governor said he would do nothing to protect them. An angry mob of more than a

thousand white people gathered outside the school to keep out the black students.

To avoid fighting and riots, Eisenhower sent army troops to keep the peace and enforce the law. With hundreds of people watching, the nine African American students walked into the high school on September 25, 1957. Many people criticized the president. Some felt he should have called in troops sooner. Others felt that he should not have become involved in local problems.

Less than two weeks later, another important event took place. On October 4, the

In 1954, the Supreme Court said that it was illegal to keep black students out of any public school. But some schools in the South refused to obey this new law. in 1957, nine students in Arkansas decided to become the first blacks to attend Central High School in Little Rock. Eisenhower worried that there would be violence. He sent troops to prevent problems, and the students arrived at the school in an army car.

Russians launched the first artificial satellite, called *Sputnik.* A month later, they launched *Sputnik II,* which carried a live dog into space. Americans were alarmed that Russia had more advanced technology than the United States. People began to question why Americans had fallen behind. Were schools not teaching enough math and science? In response, Eisenhower asked Congress to set aside more money to speed up America's space program. In three months, the United States launched its first satellite, *Explorer.*

When communist Fidel Castro became the leader of Cuba in 1959, Americans believed it was another sign that the Soviet Union was trying to take over the world. Many were frightened to have a communist country just 90 miles away, off the coast of Florida. In 1961, Eisenhower broke off diplomatic relations with Cuba. Two countries that have diplomatic relations have a friendly relationship. Representatives of each government work to create treaties and other agreements. Cuba and the United States have had no such relations since Eisenhower's presidency.

In spite of continuing problems with the Soviets, Nikita Khrushchev surprised Eisenhower by visiting the United States in 1959. Khrushchev was made to feel welcome. Despite some disagreements, the visit ended on a hopeful note. It seemed the relationship between the two countries was improving.

In the spring of 1960, representatives from the United States, the Soviet Union, Great Britain, and France planned to meet in Paris, France. Just two weeks before the meeting, the Soviets shot down an American **reconnaissance** plane over the Soviet Union.

Interesting Facts

▶ In 1959, Alaska and Hawaii became the 49th and 50th states to enter the Union.

The rise of communist leader Fidel Castro (right) on the island country of Cuba worried many Americans. Communism was closer to U.S. shores than ever before.

Soviet leader Nikita Khrushchev (right) came to the United States in 1959. He and President Eisenhower were not able to agree on every issue they discussed. Still, they ended the meeting with high hopes for better relations between the two countries. Unfortunately, these hopes were short lived. The Cold War would rage for years to come.

Eisenhower admitted that the United States had been sending spies to the region for four years, but he did not apologize. He said that if the Soviets had agreed to the Open Skies policy, there would be no need to spy. The Paris meeting fell apart after only two days.

The Cold War was worse than ever. At a United Nations meeting in 1960, the matter of the airplane was discussed. Khrushchev became so angry that he took off his shoe and pounded it on the table. Eisenhower later said that this decline in relations between the United States and the Soviet Union was the biggest disappointment of his life. His famous ability to bring people together had failed him in dealing with Khrushchev.

At the end of his second term, Eisenhower delivered a televised farewell speech to the American people. In it he said that the nation was more powerful than ever. It had a huge military force of more than three and a half million people. Factories produced large numbers of powerful weapons. He warned Americans that the great power of these forces should not be allowed to change the democratic U.S. government.

On January 20, 1961, Eisenhower passed the presidency to John F. Kennedy. Afterward, Ike and Mamie Eisenhower went to their home in Gettysburg, Pennsylvania. In his retirement, Eisenhower wrote books, painted, and played golf. Politicians continued to seek his advice and support. Years after he left office, he was still one of the most admired men in America.

Ike and Mamie Eisenhower retired to their farm in Gettysburg, Pennsylvania, after his second term ended. They enjoyed having plenty of time together. "We've always enjoyed each other's company," Mamie once said.

Dwight Eisenhower died of heart failure in 1969. Today he is remembered as a great general and a popular president. During his 50 years of service to the country, he held positions of great power. But the power itself was not important to him. He wanted to bring people together to accomplish common goals. In so doing, he changed the course of history.

WHILE MANY AMERICANS had money to spend in the 1950s, about one-fifth of the people in the United States lived in poverty. Many of these citizens were African Americans, who did not have the same opportunities that white Americans had. Although some laws that **discriminated** against African Americans had been changed, they often were not enforced. During the 1950s, people began to fight this discrimination more than ever before.

In 1954, the Supreme Court ruled that public schools had to be integrated. In 1955, Dr. Martin Luther King Jr. helped organize peaceful demonstrations against discrimination in Montgomery, Alabama. A demonstration is when a group of people with a common goal or belief participate in a march, rally, or other public action to show their support for a cause. Soon there were demonstrations in many parts of the South. For years, white people in the South had tried to keep blacks from voting. In 1957, President Eisenhower signed a law to protect the right to vote for all Americans.

Not everyone was happy with these changes. Some people believed that blacks did not deserve equal rights. The women in this photograph are shown picketing in front of their children's school. They were angry that blacks were allowed to attend classes with their children.

The fight for equal rights for all American citizens was called the Civil Rights Movement. Although it gained more attention in the 1960s, its beginnings were in the 1950s, when some Americans were left out of the nation's new prosperity.

1890 David Dwight Eisenhower is born on October 14 in Denison, Texas.

1891 Eisenhower moves with his family to Abilene, Kansas.

1909 Eisenhower changes his name to Dwight David.

1911 Eisenhower enters West Point Military Academy.

1915 Eisenhower graduates from West Point. He is assigned to Fort Sam Houston in Texas.

1916 Eisenhower marries Mamie Geneva Doud on July 1.

1918 The army sends Eisenhower to Camp Colt in Pennsylvania as the commanding officer of the Tank Training Center. He is in charge of 6,000 men.

1919 Eisenhower is ordered to Camp Meade to command a series of heavy tank battalions.

1921 Eisenhower graduates from Tank School at Camp Meade and is placed in command of the 301st Tank battalion.

1922 Eisenhower becomes executive officer for the 20th Infantry Brigade in the Panama Canal Zone.

1933 Eisenhower becomes an assistant to General Douglas MacArthur, who is chief of staff of the U.S. Army.

1935 Eisenhower is named senior assistant to General MacArthur, now military advisor to the Philippines.

1936 Germany, Japan, and Italy join forces to form the Axis powers.

1939 Germany takes over Czechoslovakia and invades Poland. World War II begins.

1940 Eisenhower returns to the United States from the Philippines.

1941 Japan bombs Pearl Harbor on December 7. Eisenhower is assigned to Washington, D.C., as the assistant chief of staff of the War Plans Division.

1942 Eisenhower is appointed commander of European operations and sent to London. He commands the Allied invasion of North Africa on November 8.

1943 Eisenhower directs the invasion of Italy. He is promoted to the rank of brigadier general and then major general. On December 24, he is appointed supreme commander of the Allied Forces.

1944 Eisenhower directs "Operation Overlord," the invasion of France, on June 6. In less than one year, the Allies successfully push the Nazis back to Germany.

1945 Germany surrenders to the Allies on May 7. The United States drops atomic bombs on Japan in August. Japan surrenders and World War II ends. President Truman names Eisenhower chief of staff of the U.S. Army.

1948 Eisenhower resigns as chief of staff. Later that year, he becomes president of Columbia University.

1950 President Truman appoints Eisenhower supreme commander of the North Atlantic Treaty Organization (NATO).

1952 Eisenhower is elected president of the United States. He visits Korea before he takes office.

1953 Eisenhower becomes the 34th president of the United States on January 20.

1955 Eisenhower attends the Geneva Summit Conference in July to meet with the leaders of France, Great Britain, and the Soviet Union. In September, he has a heart attack in Denver, Colorado.

1956 Eisenhower is elected to a second term in November.

1957 In March, the Eisenhower Doctrine Bill is signed. In September, Eisenhower sends U.S. Army troops to Little Rock to uphold a Supreme Court order to integrate public schools. The Russians launch the satellite *Sputnik* in October.

1958 The first U.S. satellite, *Explorer,* is launched in January.

1959 Soviet leader Nikita Khrushchev visits the United States. Alaska and Hawaii become the 49th and 50th states.

1960 A U.S. reconnaissance plane is shot down over Russia. The Paris Summit meeting between NATO countries and the Soviet Union collapses after two days.

1961 Eisenhower breaks diplomatic relations with Cuba. On January 20, he leaves office. He retires with Mamie to their farm in Gettysburg, Pennsylvania.

1969 Eisenhower dies on March 28 in Walter Reed Army Medical Center in Washington, D.C. He is 78 years old.

allies (AL-lize)
Allies are nations that have agreed to help each other by fighting together against a common enemy. During World War II, the countries that fought against the Germans were called the Allies.

atomic bombs (uh-TOM-ik BOMZ)
Atomic bombs are a type of bomb that causes a very powerful, hot explosion and terrible destruction. The war with Japan ended after the United States dropped atomic bombs.

bill (BILL)
A bill is an idea for a new law that is presented to a group of lawmakers. President Eisenhower urged Congress to pass a bill that would allow Americans to pay fewer taxes.

candidate (KAN-dih-det)
A candidate is a person running in an election. Eisenhower agreed to become a presidential candidate in 1952.

censure (SEN-shur)
If the Senate censures a politician, its members state that they think he or she has done something wrong. The Senate censured Joseph McCarthy in 1954.

communism (KOM-yeh-niz-em)
Communism is a system of government in which the central government, not the people, hold all the power, and there is no private ownership of property. During the Cold War, a major goal of Soviet leaders was to spread communism throughout the world.

democracies (deh-MOK-reh-seez)
Democracies are nations in which the people control the government by electing their own leaders. The United States is a democracy.

discriminate (dih-SKRIM-ih-nayt)
If people discriminate against others, they treat them unfairly simply because they are different. The Civil Rights Movement began in the 1950s to fight discrimination.

integrated (IN-teh-gray-ted)
If something is integrated, it can be used equally by all people. In 1954, the Supreme Court ruled that public schools must be integrated.

maneuvers (meh-NOO-verz)
Maneuvers are military exercises that soldiers practice to prepare for war. Eisenhower was in charge of training troops and practicing maneuvers.

occupied (AHK-yeh-pied)
An occupied country is one that has been taken over by another country. During World War II, occupied France was controlled by Germany.

political party (puh-LIT-ih-kul PAR-tee)
A political party is a group of people who share similar ideas about how to run a government. Germany's Nazi political party came to power in the 1930s.

promoted (pruh-MOH-ted)
People who are promoted receive a more important job or position to recognize their good work. Eisenhower was so good at military work that he was promoted many times.

racial (RAY-shul)
Racial means having to do with people's races. When African Americans began to demand equal rights, it caused racial tension between blacks and whites in the South.

reconnaissance (ree-KAH-nuh-sentz)
Reconnaissance is the inspection or exploration of an area, especially to gather information about military forces. The United States flew reconnaissance missions over the Soviet Union for years during the Cold War.

strategy (STRAT-eh-jee)
Strategy is the science of planning and directing military movements and operations. Eisenhower worked with other military leaders on the strategy to invade Italy in 1943.

taxes (TAK-sez)
Taxes are payments citizens make to help support a government. With lower taxes in the 1950s, people had more money to spend on products.

term (TERM)
A term is the length of time a politician can keep his or her position by law. A U.S. president's term is four years.

tuition (too-ISH-un)
Tuition is the fee for going to a school. When Eisenhower graduated from high school, he couldn't afford the tuition for college.

Our Presidents

President	Birthplace	Life Span	Presidency	Political Party	First Lady
George Washington	Virginia	1732–1799	1789–1797	None	Martha Dandridge Custis Washington
John Adams	Massachusetts	1735–1826	1797–1801	Federalist	Abigail Smith Adams
Thomas Jefferson	Virginia	1743–1826	1801–1809	Democratic-Republican	widower
James Madison	Virginia	1751–1836	1809–1817	Democratic Republican	Dolley Payne Todd Madison
James Monroe	Virginia	1758–1831	1817–1825	Democratic Republican	Elizabeth Kortright Monroe
John Quincy Adams	Massachusetts	1767–1848	1825–1829	Democratic-Republican	Louisa Johnson Adams
Andrew Jackson	South Carolina	1767–1845	1829–1837	Democrat	widower
Martin Van Buren	New York	1782–1862	1837–1841	Democrat	widower
William H. Harrison	Virginia	1773–1841	1841	Whig	Anna Symmes Harrison
John Tyler	Virginia	1790–1862	1841–1845	Whig	Letitia Christian Tyler / Julia Gardiner Tyler
James K. Polk	North Carolina	1795–1849	1845–1849	Democrat	Sarah Childress Polk

President	Birthplace	Life Span	Presidency	Political Party	First Lady
Zachary Taylor	Virginia	1784–1850	1849–1850	Whig	Margaret Mackall Smith Taylor
Millard Fillmore	New York	1800–1874	1850–1853	Whig	Abigail Powers Fillmore
Franklin Pierce	New Hampshire	1804–1869	1853–1857	Democrat	Jane Means Appleton Pierce
James Buchanan	Pennsylvania	1791–1868	1857–1861	Democrat	never married
Abraham Lincoln	Kentucky	1809–1865	1861–1865	Republican	Mary Todd Lincoln
Andrew Johnson	North Carolina	1808–1875	1865–1869	Democrat	Eliza McCardle Johnson
Ulysses S. Grant	Ohio	1822–1885	1869–1877	Republican	Julia Dent Grant
Rutherford B. Hayes	Ohio	1822–1893	1877–1881	Republican	Lucy Webb Hayes
James A. Garfield	Ohio	1831–1881	1881	Republican	Lucretia Rudolph Garfield
Chester A. Arthur	Vermont	1829–1886	1881–1885	Republican	widower
Grover Cleveland	New Jersey	1837–1908	1885–1889	Democrat	Frances Folsom Cleveland

President	Birthplace	Life Span	Presidency	Political Party	First Lady
Benjamin Harrison	Ohio	1833–1901	1889–1893	Republican	Caroline Scott Harrison
Grover Cleveland	New Jersey	1837–1908	1893–1897	Democrat	Frances Folsom Cleveland
William McKinley	Ohio	1843–1901	1897–1901	Republican	Ida Saxton McKinley
Theodore Roosevelt	New York	1858–1919	1901–1909	Republican	Edith Kermit Carow Roosevelt
William H. Taft	Ohio	1857–1930	1909–1913	Republican	Helen Herron Taft
Woodrow Wilson	Virginia	1856–1924	1913–1921	Democrat	Ellen L. Axson Wilson Edith Bolling Galt Wilson
Warren G. Harding	Ohio	1865–1923	1921–1923	Republican	Florence Kling De Wolfe Harding
Calvin Coolidge	Vermont	1872–1933	1923–1929	Republican	Grace Goodhue Coolidge
Herbert C. Hoover	Iowa	1874–1964	1929–1933	Republican	Lou Henry Hoover
Franklin D. Roosevelt	New York	1882–1945	1933–1945	Democrat	Anna Eleanor Roosevelt Roosevelt
Harry S. Truman	Missouri	1884–1972	1945–1953	Democrat	Elizabeth Wallace Truman

Our PRESIDENTS

President	Birthplace	Life Span	Presidency	Political Party	First Lady
Dwight D. Eisenhower	Texas	1890–1969	1953–1961	Republican	Mary "Mamie" Doud Eisenhower
John F. Kennedy	Massachusetts	1917–1963	1961–1963	Democrat	Jacqueline Bouvier Kennedy
Lyndon B. Johnson	Texas	1908–1973	1963–1969	Democrat	Claudia Alta Taylor Johnson
Richard M. Nixon	California	1913–1994	1969–1974	Republican	Thelma Catherine Ryan Nixon
Gerald Ford	Nebraska	1913–	1974–1977	Republican	Elizabeth "Betty" Bloomer Warren Ford
James Carter	Georgia	1924–	1977–1981	Democrat	Rosalynn Smith Carter
Ronald Reagan	Illinois	1911–	1981–1989	Republican	Nancy Davis Reagan
George Bush	Massachusetts	1924–	1989–1993	Republican	Barbara Pierce Bush
William Clinton	Arkansas	1946–	1993–2001	Democrat	Hillary Rodham Clinton
George W. Bush	Connecticut	1946–	2001–	Republican	Laura Welch Bush

Presidential FACTS

Qualifications

To run for president, a candidate must

- be at least 35 years old
- be a citizen who was born in the United States
- have lived in the United States for 14 years

Term of Office

A president's term of office is four years. No president can stay in office for more than two terms.

Election Date

The presidential election takes place every four years on the first Tuesday of November.

Inauguration Date

Presidents are inaugurated on January 20.

Oath of Office

I do solemnly swear I will faithfully execute the office of the President of the United States and will to the best of my ability preserve, protect, and defend the Constitution of the United States.

Write a Letter to the President

One of the best things about being a U.S. citizen is that Americans get to participate in their government. They can speak out if they feel government leaders aren't doing their jobs. They can also praise leaders who are going the extra mile. Do you have something you'd like the president to do? Should the president worry more about the environment and encourage people to recycle? Should the government spend more money on our schools? You can write a letter to the president to say how you feel!

1600 Pennsylvania Avenue
Washington, D.C. 20500

You can even send an e-mail to: president@whitehouse.gov

For Further INFORMATION

Internet Sites

Learn more about President Eisenhower:
http://www.whitehouse.gov/WH/glimpse/presidents/htm/d34.html

Visit Eisenhower's birthplace:
http://www.eisenhowerbirthplace.org/

Visit the Eisenhower Library:
http://redbud.lbjlib.utexas.edu/eisenhower/

Find out more about World War II:
http://grolier.com/wwii/wwii_2.html

Study the 1959 meeting between Khrushchev and Eisenhower at Gettysburg:
http://www.cr.nps.gov/hr/twhp/wwwlps/lessons/29ike.htm

Learn more about all the presidents and visit the White House:
http://www.whitehouse.gov/WH/glimpse/presidents/html/presidents.html
http://www.thepresidency.org/presinfo.htm
http://www.americanpresidents.org/

Books

Beschloss, Michael R. *Mayday.* New York: Harper and Row, 1986.

Cannon, Marion G. *Dwight David Eisenhower, War Hero and President.* New York: Franklin Watts, 1990.

Steins, Richard. *The Allies against the Axis: World War II (1940–1950).* New York: Twenty-First Century Books, 1995.

Van Steenwyk, Elizabeth. *Dwight David Eisenhower, President.* New York: Walker and Company, 1987.

Warren, James A. *Cold War: The American Crusade against the Soviet Union and World Communism, 1945–1990.* New York: Lothrop, Lee & Shepard, 1996.

Zeinert, Karen. *McCarthy and the Fear of Communism in American History.* Springfield, NJ: Enslow Publishers, 1998.

Index